MW01123531

A Year in Union Square

52 *Seasonal Pasta Dishes*

A Year in Union Square

52 *Seasonal Pasta Dishes*

by
Eileen Gardiner
& Ron Musto

PIERREPONT
STREET PRESS
NEW YORK
2015

Copyright © 2015 by Pierrepont Street Press

ITALICA PRESS, INC.

595 Main Street

New York, New York 10044

inquiries@italicapress.com

Pierrepont Street Press is a registered imprint of Italica Press, Inc. All rights reserved. No part of this publication may be reproduced, stored in a retrieval system, or transmitted, in any form or by any means, electronic, mechanical, photocopying, recording or otherwise, without prior permission of Italica Press. For permission to reproduce selected portions, please contact the Press at inquiries@italicapress.com.

Library of Congress Cataloging-in-Publication Data

Gardiner, Eileen.

A year in Union Square : 52 seasonal pasta dishes / by Eileen Gardiner & Ron Musto.

  pages cm

Includes index.

Summary: "Presents 52 pasta recipes drawn from family, Italian and southern French cuisines, following each week of the year. These recipes trace the turning seasons and use the weekly vegetables and produce, fish, meats and dairy at New York's Union Square Greenmarket. Includes introduction, indexes and a photo of each dish"— Provided by publisher.

ISBN 978-1-59910-317-4 (hardcover : alk. paper) — ISBN 978-1-59910-318-1 (pbk. : alk. paper) — ISBN 978-1-59910-319-8 (e-book)

  1. Cooking (Pasta) 2. Seasonal cooking—New York (State)—New York. 3. Union Square (New York, N.Y.) I. Musto, Ronald G. II. Title.

TX809.M17G37 2015

641.82'2—dc23

2015034333

Cover image: *Fifty-Two Pasta Dishes.* Composite image of photos taken 2013–2015, imported into iPhoto and screen captured. © Italica Press 2015.

FOR A COMPLETE LIST OF ITALICA PRESS TITLES

VISIT OUR WEB SITE AT:

WWW.ITALICAPRESS.COM

Contents

A Year in Union Square

Illustrations

All illustrations © Italica Press. Pasta images taken with Apple iPad A1430. Images of Union Square and Greenmarket taken with Olympus E-620 system, Canon Elph 520 HS and Apple iPhone 5S.

Introduction

Fresh Asparagus

It was 1982 and we'd just moved back to New York City after a few years of academic wandering, leaving Brooklyn Heights for Rome (Italy), Cambridge (MA) and Durham (NC). When we'd left the Heights our rent was $235/mo. for a lovely one-bedroom with working fireplace and a view of the harbor. When we returned to New York, those rents had just added a zero at the end. Now we wanted to live in Manhattan and found that our budget would only allow us to take up the pioneer's life in a converted office building on East 22nd Street, just behind the Flatiron Building.

It's hard to imagine it now, but back then there were only a few residential buildings in the East 20s west of Gramercy Park, few retail stores off Fifth Avenue and no food shopping to speak of west of Second Avenue. We'd never been in this situation before, not even in car-only Durham, NC (where we'd grocery shopped on our bicycles). Ever since we were young kids growing up in Brooklyn there had always been the corner grocer selling everything from artichokes to stiff bacala in open barrels, butcher shops, fish stores, bakeries, and special fruit and vegetable markets. Ralph the vegetable man and his horse Babe would come by twice a week with their wagon, Ralph shouting out the latest price of fresh asparagus as they approached.

Summers in Rocky Point, Long Island for Ron brought dirt, then tar, roads and walks to the local farm for milk, cream and eggs. Farm stands lined Route 25A selling their produce: corn, potatoes, strawberries, peaches. Summer days also brought awed silence as Don Antonio, our Nonna Casolaro's neighbor across the road, expounded on zucchini and their blossoms (*sciarille* or *fior' di zucca*), the long green squash he called *cucuzille,* string beans off the pole, peppers, onions and, most of all, tomatoes off the vine, all loaded into our arms by Tony's daughter Lulu and sent back with us in abundance. Behind that bungalow Ron's grandmother's garden (and her grandchildren's labor) produced grapes, tomatoes and other vegetables, but nothing like Don Antonio's. *Maestra* of a sophisticated household back in New York, "up in the country" Nonna specialized in more wild fare: after every major rain she would take us — one, two or a dozen siblings and cousins, whoever happened to be there that week — hunting through Rocky Point's sandy pine and oak forests for fresh, wild mushrooms. Avoid the red ones, the ones with dips in the center, the ones next to rusty cans or the ones on newly mown lawns with dogs. The taste of fresh wild mushrooms, sautéed with oil and garlic…. Those taste memories set us all on a life-long search for good food and ingredients.

By her own admission, Eileen's family did not start out as pasta cooks, but for some reason her father took a real interest in Italian food. He loved to go to the Italian butcher, and he pioneered several pasta recipes, which gave her an early understanding of the good and the bad. One of her earliest memories was being made to sit at the table and finish her spaghetti before being allowed to watch some program or other on TV. The Gardiners often had a homemade tomato sauce, so bitter that it hurt the mouth. Her father's cooking improved though, and by the time she was a teenager he had pretty much perfected, after a fashion, four recipes involving four different pastas: baked ziti and cheese, spaghetti and meatballs (or sausage), linguine with clam sauce and ravioli with tomato sauce. The

Gardiner kids used to get sent to Maresca's Grocery Store in Cobble Hill where they would buy their *pasta secca* by number: 2, 8 and 17 respectively. The ravioli were always fresh: Bruno's large cheese. After Eileen met Ron, he soon pronounced her father's cooking "tasty," which became a long-standing family joke. Then her father met Ron's mother, who taught him how to make octopus Neapolitan style! Many family dinners at the Mustos with the Gardiners followed.

Dyker Heights and Carroll Gardens were full of open-air vegetable stands run by Italians. When we met in college at Fordham in the Bronx, Arthur Avenue in the Wedge — as the Italian neighborhood south of Fordham Road was called — was, and still is, full of open-air Italian markets and an indoor city market. They sold and still sell everything from vegetables and fruits to fish, shellfish, meats and cold cuts, cheeses, olives and stuffed peppers, olive oils, coffees, wines, breads, pastries, pizza, nuts, dried fruits, and on and on....

After college, during the Vietnam War and our two-year stint in Boston while Ron served as a conscientious objector, we lived on Beacon Hill and would stroll or roll our bikes down to the Haymarket. There we found a student's and minimum-wage-earners' heaven of fruits and vegetables, meats, cheeses, dairy: 3 pounds of sausage for $1.00, 3 dozen pullet eggs for $1.00, roast beefs for $3.00, pounds of peaches, broccoli, artichokes for under $2.00....

When we returned to New York and graduate school at Columbia and CUNY, life on Morningside Heights seemed a bit sterile. So we headed back to the neighborhood where Eileen had grown up and found ourselves in that $235/mo. apartment on Pierrepont Street, a half-block from the

Brooklyn Heights Promenade. Here we did our dissertation
writing and launched Pierrepont Street Press: a "hot type"
house with a few metal fonts and a small hand press. Now
every week included a bike ride or walk to Carroll Gardens
where we gradually found acceptance — and a recognized
place in line — at the local bakery, butcher, fish shop, vegetable and cheese and specialty stores. Atlantic Avenue offered
the welcome and exotic variety of Sahadi Grocery, Damascus
Bakery and Oriental Pastry and Grocery. On the north end
of the Heights, almost at the end of Henry Street, a young
couple usually in denim overalls, combat boots and dreadlocks
had opened a fresh produce store in a barely renovated corner
storefront, one of the earliest organic markets around. But even
in the mid-1970s some things were still hard to find. One had
to ride into Manhattan, to 9th Avenue, to find bunches of fresh
basil for an off-season pesto.

Graduate school brought yearly summer travel for research to
Italy and the UK. A summer spent in Florence in 1974, living
on Borgo degli Albizzi, included daily strolls to the Mercato
del Porcellino (back then selling cut flowers along with the
leather goods), to the market outside San Lorenzo or to the
indoor Mercato Centrale. Outside our windows on Borgo
degli Albizzi, every morning and lunch, a street vendor would
ladle up fresh, fragrant tripe — in its own steaming juices or in
tomato sauce — on hard crusty rolls. In the Mercato Centrale
a tiny lunch counter just inside the doors, always packed with
workers from the stalls, specialized in the same, but the market
itself was a wonder of fresh produce, meats, fish…. Those taste
and smell memories are hard to forget.

Summers in and around London's Bloomsbury during the
1970s were great for access to the British Library but meant

something else again for food, until friends and colleagues did manage to steer us toward cheeses, dairy and fresh meats and produce at the shops on Lamb's Conduit and off the Angel in Islington.

With a year at the American Academy in Rome during 1978/79 and in many later residences in that city we took full advantage of the markets in Campo dei Fiori, Testaccio and Piazza Vittorio Emmanuele for fish, meat, vegetables, fruits, nuts, herbs and spices. Travel through Italy had also brought us to the wonders of meat, fish and vegetable markets in Venice, Verona, Palermo, Naples and Milan. Years later, during a semester spent at the American Academy in 1993/94, we shopped regularly at the via Niccolini market on Monteverde Vecchio and learned, the hard way, about the loyalty given to — and expected by — Italian vendors and their market customers. Since then we've had the chance of visiting and shopping in markets in Paris, Arles, Barcelona, Istanbul, Bergama, Amsterdam, Los Angeles, St. Louis, Montreal and Toronto, and at the two fledgling farmers' markets around Harvard Square in Cambridge, MA. No wonder East 22nd Street came as a shock way back then.

The Union Square Market
One day in 1982 we read a notice that in 1976 Union Square had begun a limited experiment in what they were calling the Farmer's Greenmarket. A few growers from the Hudson Valley and one of two from New Jersey had been persuaded by the city and a committee of citizens to come to Union Square on Saturdays to set up booths and to try to sell their produce. The farmers were doing whatever they could to reach new markets to survive and grow, while the city was attempting to bring

normal activity and new residents to what was a deserted and drug-ridden park and neighborhood.

So we started shopping at Union Square. Back in the early 80s the choices weren't very broad: mostly apples, pears, cabbages, potatoes, onions, carrots, broccoli and a few other standard crops grown around New York. Shopping in the Market was more an act of faith and support than a real convenience or a magnet for special foods. Gradually, however, that began to change. As the Market gained more and more attention and customers, farmers began to respond to customers' requests: broccoli and potatoes made room for broccoli rabe, arugula, basil, garlic, heirloom tomatoes, zucchini and their blossoms, asparagus, then berries in season, everything from strawberries to blue, black and raspberries. Fish, poultry and meat stalls multiplied. Dairy stands started selling milk, cream, yogurt, fruit drinks. They were joined by makers of cheese, baked goods, granola, pretzels and fine breads, flours and beans. By the early 2000s the Market was setting trends for New York: ramps and morels, fiddleheads, spring garlic, snap peas, heirlooms, artichokes, edible blossoms filled the booths next to cooking classes, community outreach and a thriving and real organic movement.

The young children of the first farm vendors reached adulthood, and then started selling at the Market with their own children, their nieces and nephews. Many original farmers starting coming with newly hired staff, and soon some staff replaced the original owners either as sales people or as owners themselves. The Saturday market was gradually supplemented by Wednesdays and Fridays and by a Monday organic-only market. Early morning shoppers eventually had the company of restaurant buyers, usually coming to the Market with small carts or specialty bicycles made for loading produce, often snapping up a farmer's entire day's offering of asparagus or ramps, morels or steamer clams.

Name Dropping

It's often said that Union Square and its reputation as a food center was put on the map by Danny Meyer and his Union Square Cafe. But the Market had nearly a full decade on the 1985 founding of that restaurant, and by then the square had already become a destination for day-to-day shoppers. Union Square had long been a center for NYU and for publishers — everyone from NYU Press and Farrar, Straus & Giroux to Hill & Wang, Rowman & Littlefield, St. Martin's, Springer Verlag, Plenum, Houghton-Mifflin Harcourt and their lunching editors and authors. A few blocks west along Fifth and Sixth Avenues, the old printer's district had been replaced by the new computer district: IT and "desktop" publishing, fashion photography and design. So the combination of culture workers and the proximity of good, fresh foods made it a natural location for fine and innovative chefs. Still, it would take a few more years and a few more restaurants — including the Gotham Bar & Grill, the Gramercy Tavern, the Blue Water Grill, the Mesa Grill, City Bakery and Casa Mono — to make it the foodie paradise it would become. Since then Union Square and its Greenmarket has taken its place among the great markets of the country and the world.

So, long after we'd moved from 22nd Street to Roosevelt Island in search of space, views and quiet, we too continued to make the subway or bus trip down for our weekly stock. One night at a gala given in New York by the American Academy in Rome, we had the good fortune to be seated with Academy

trustees Andrew Heiskell and Mrs. Heiskell — née Marian
Sulzberger. Ron was serving on the board of the Academy
alumni association as editor of its *Society of Fellows News* and
had just written and run a story on Mr. Heiskell — which
he liked — and so that and the fact that our family business
(Italica Press) and theirs (Time Inc., *The New York Times*) had
"publishing" in common made for some brief but delicate
conversation. Talk soon turned to the safe zones of Naples —
where Mr. Heiskell had been born and whose dialect he spoke
— and of food, a favorite among *Italianisti*, and so on to the
Union Square Greenmarket. On firmer ground now, Ron began to describe in great detail the Market's recent renovations
and alterations to its ground plan, wondering aloud if these
would substantially harm the feel of the place. Mrs. Heiskell
thought not, and very politely went on to inform Ron of her
founding role in the creation of the Greenmarket and of her
continued hand in its current renovation, which, we all soon
concluded, was a good thing.

Why Union Square Matters

Foodies and fashionable restaurants, organic and fresh produce,
farm-fresh eggs, beef and poultry are all fine, but they come
at a price: the Greenmarket's offerings can be more expensive
than supermarket fare; and many friends and neighbors declare
that they see little reason to spend so much for the same foods.
But are they the same? And is shopping at Union Square simply a matter of food snobbery or trendy consumerism?

One of the major reasons why the original farmers accepted
the invitation to come down or over to Union Square was
very simple economics: coming out of the 1960s and into the
recession of the 1970s, faced by the growing corporatization of

the food industry, west-coast and foreign imports of cheap produce, and the continued encroachment of suburbs and industry into farmlands, the remaining farmers of the Hudson Valley and New Jersey were looking for new markets. It was not a matter of chic or extra profit. They brought those first truck-loads of potatoes, carrots, cabbages and eggs because it made good sense: to expand markets and to preserve livelihoods handed down to them by their parents and grandparents. Nor were the first Union Square customers looking to spot the latest *Gourmet* or *Saveur* trendings: they too recognized the value of fresh food and of dealing direct with their producers. Union Square has always been a focus of alterative politics and culture, and the addition of a new food counterculture was a welcome sign of renewal.

As the Market became established and more farmers and more produce began to fill the stalls, this initial impetus began to have a very real impact: Hudson Valley farms not only survived, they began to thrive, and then to multiply, giving rise to any number of local food cultures and economies from High Falls to Rhinebeck. "Expensive" food became a real alternative to corporate "feed-lot" culture, and a respect for the farmers and their workers, for their animals and for their produce became less a chic fetish and more a path to market independence, local economy and the personal relationships around food and eating. Knowing and chatting with your local farmer on a weekly basis restored the relationship to food and its growers that many of us remember from our days in neighborhoods, in the country, in European and other markets.

Buying from farmers whom you knew and to whom you will return weekly also guarantees that quality will remain high. Unlike factory farms and processors, Greenmarket

farmers do not need to issue recalls on everything from
chopped meat to cucumbers. The extra benefits are well worth
the added price. But cheaper corporate produce has its price
too: it is raised in conditions of questionable health and safety,
transported hundreds or thousands of miles, consuming fossil
fuels, roads and warehouses, treated with who knows what
chemicals (and GMOs) for growing and long storage, increas-
ingly tainted by salmonella and other poor-handling problems,
discounted and short-priced to farmers to insure huge volume
— and profit — to a few mega food corporations.

Local farming and markets suddenly reverse all of the market
equations established in the 1950s and 60s. Good food goes to
customers. Sustainability and profit go to local farmers and their
families and workers. Both feed local economies with a sustainable and health-giving exchange. Market stalls have long accepted Food Stamps, EBT/FMNP and other food supplement
programs, and as the years have gone on more and more people
with low incomes have been able to buy and eat well because of
the Greenmarket. Unsold food donations to City Harvest and
the NYC Coalition Against Hunger increase yearly too.

"You know that what you eat you are" sing the Beatles, and
this well expresses the traditional connection between mi-
crocosm and macrocosm. Making the world a better place is
directly and intimately linked to making your own body and
life more whole and healthy, both less dependent on artificial stimulations, artificial sustainability, both less the object of
corporate profit schemes that turn humans themselves into
produce and their eating lives into feed lots.

The benefits of eating both locally and seasonably also put
shoppers directly into touch with the cycle of the seasons.

Fresh raspberries do not grow here in November. To get them we have to rely on underpaid, badly treated migrants in the Sun Belt, fossil-fueled trucks and their drivers traveling thousands of miles, storage and preservative systems that add immense social and economic costs to such normal luxuries. Inexpensive chicken and beef, animal life sold cheaper than supermarket broccoli, is not worth the documented horrors of caged living, torturous treatment and factory processing. For most of us paying more also means both eating less (a good thing for individuals, America and the globe) and buying from suppliers who treat their little part of the earth, its produce and its animals with a new humane standard that is both sustainable and just. Eating with the seasons also provides our bodies with varying nutrients, tastes and textures that we need as sunlight, temperature and weather vary over the course of the year. It also makes us conscious of change and of our choices. You know that what you eat you are.

The Idea of this Book

But enough food preaching. We wrote this little book for the fun of it. It was first a series of 52 weekly posts on Facebook; and friends and family asked for more. We can't think of any food we enjoy cooking and eating more than pasta, and we can't imagine a better place to do our shopping than here in New York City. We're not saying that the dishes we present here are all that we eat, or are all the possible pasta recipes we can cook, or are all the foods that one can buy in New York, and even all the foods available at the Union Square Greenmarket. But they are what we thought were the best pasta recipes to match what was available in the Market for any given week as the year progressed. This sometimes ranged from very little at all to so many choices that we had to pick our ingredients carefully so as not to repeat or overlap dishes. Some produce, such as fresh asparagus or peas, are so special when they arrive at the Market that we've presented several different ways of making them with different pastas. Some of the pastas themselves repeat many times throughout these pages, and this is mostly because the Market offers fewer choices than, say, Eataly opposite the Flatiron Building, Buon'Italia at Chelsea Market off the High Line or Raffetto's on Houston Street.

Recipes are organized first by season, then by week through each month, and we've picked the number of weeks for each month for a "typical" year. Recipes follow this seasonal and weekly availability. We had no set ideas when we'd set out for the Market any particular morning: the recipes that emerged were based on what we could find — usually around some main ingredient, often supplemented by others from other sources when the Market choices were few. So we've omitted many dishes we, and you, often make that use main ingredients we could not find at Union Square. Sometimes, rarely, we used other ingredients if the main ingredients were found at the Market and we could not resist doing an old standard or trying something new. But the main idea was to present simple recipes that highlight the main one or two ingredients in as straightforward a way as possible. That, we've come to understand, is the essence of the best Italian regional cooking.

These recipes are generally vegetarian, sometimes vegan, and pancetta or guanciale can be removed from most of these dishes, a little butter substituted for vegetarians or omitted for vegans. Many of these dishes show our preference for southern Italian cooking, but many are most definitely from other parts of Italy: Lazio and Rome, Tuscany, Liguria. Those who prefer the cooking of the Veneto and le Marche may also find some traces here. As we've gotten older we've definitely developed a preference for less meat. Long gone are the days when, pencil thin, we would roll down Beacon Hill on our bikes to buy 3 pounds of sausage for $1.00 and consume it all within 3 days. Age, health, animal welfare, micro- and macrocosmic considerations have all played a role. Our non-vegetarian recipes show a decided preference for fish; and although the Market now has several growers of excellent beef, pork, lamb and poultry, except for holidays we now rarely buy and make these at home, and rarely make pasta recipes containing them. There are exceptions, and every so often that Neapolitan *vouli* for an old family recipe can't be resisted. We hope we've presented enough recipes and range to please every approach to our readers' eating and cooking.

The Organization of this Book
Each of the following recipes is presented on a two-page spread. A photo of the finished dish is on the left, always at the same size; and the recipe is on the facing, odd-numbered page. Each recipe page presents the same format: the month and week number, the recipe name (usually a pasta with its main ingredients), an ingredients header followed by the ingredients listed in two columns in order of their addition to the pan. The recipe follows, usually in a single paragraph and often containing many standard formulas for each process. We assume that readers are familiar with basic cooking methods and measurements or that, if not, they can find these in many classic cook books, TV shows or videos. In the Appendix we have, however, listed some standard ingredients and cooking methods, and we have indicated these by setting the ingredient, such as ARTICHOKES, in small caps.

Unlike so many pasta cookbooks, we've used a small format. This book measures only about 5 x 8 inches. We did this for two reasons: first to make it and its color reproductions less expensive to produce and buy; and second (and more important) so that you can carry it with you on trips to your local farmer's market, following the seasons and their changing produce. This is a book meant for both reading indoors and for picking fresh foods in open-air markets.

We've also included several organizing and finding tools: the table of contents lists recipes by season and week. The indexes provide ingredients alphabetically by pasta, then by main ingredients. Unless they are a main ingredient or a different variety, we haven't indexed items like olive oil, pepperoncini, salt & pepper, garlic, parsley, etc., since these appear in almost every recipe.

Methods & Equipment
We're two home cooks, and we're sure professional chefs and those who've studied their methods can improve on these recipes in any number if ways. Our intent here is just to show the possibilities of dishes that can be made with these ingredients and how we've gone about doing that. Our main influences have been home, family and Italian and southern French cooking.

We don't own a TV, and while we've watched lots of cooking shows in hotel rooms and at family and friends — and we appreciate good technique — we don't claim to have or offer any. We're never in any hurry to slice, dice or chop, and we cook for the pleasure of it, taking time with the ingredients. We're not cooking for a restaurant full of hungry and demanding patrons, and our dinner parties are usually six to eight people. Most of the recipes here are intended for two to four servings: two if these are dinner, four as a smaller first course followed by a *secondo*.

Our equipment is pretty simple: an array of IKEA, All-Clad, and Cuisinart pans and covers, including four high-walled (3-inch tall) sauté pans (two 10-inch, two 13-inch wide); a large (4-quart) and small (10-cup) pasta pot; a mini Cuisinart blender; two sets of Good Grips "Professional" knives, plus an assortment of peeling, shelling, paring and other smaller knives mainly from Williams Sonoma and Pottery Barn; about a dozen wooden cutting and serving boards; wooden spoons, forks, mixing and serving pieces (many inherited from Ron's mom, many others bought over the years and properly browned and burnt); sea salt and white and black pepper mills; a few dozen jars of herbs and spices and a hanging assortment of garden-fresh herbs; about a dozen types of dried pasta *(pasta secca)* in clasped pantry jars (Fido, Le Parfait, IKEA); some no-scratch ladles and slotted and sauce spoons. We have no special refrigerator or deep freeze, no kitchen island or chef's pantry, no professional stove top, although we do cook with gas.

Basic Ingredients & Approaches

These recipes are for two to four servings and use about 6½ ounces of pasta. We generally don't use set-in-stone measurements: use your own experience, sense of taste and proportion. You'll see that most of these recipes call for very few — but mostly fresh — ingredients. Unless otherwise specified, almost all of these recipes assume the use of olive oil (clear, not *vergine*), milled sea salt & pepper (black or white as specified), pepperoncini (whole or in flakes), fresh cloves of garlic (not powder) and herbs picked fresh from our garden or bought at

the Greenmarket (not bottled from the supermarket). We salt
our pasta water with sea salt as soon as we turn on the heat.
We use pecorino in these recipes where we might just as well
use Parmigiano: the reason is that several farm stands now sell
locally made pecorino, but Parmigiano is, after all, Parmigiano.
If you like more or less garlic, do add or subtract it. If you don't
like garlic at all, there's a lovely Time-Life cookbook entitled
The Cooking of the British Isles from 1969 that you'll enjoy.

Above all, don't over-sauce. The recipes usually call for much
of the sauce liquid to be absorbed into the pasta and for the
finished pasta to glisten with the cooking oils. Trust us here, or
remember your own experience dining in Italy.

In the Appendix (page 113) we've included a set of recipes or
preparation methods for standard ingredients used frequently
in these recipes. Again, these are indicated by the type set in
small caps, such as ARTICHOKES.

All measurements are US: quarts, cups, pounds, ounces,
inches, etc. Appendix 2 (page 120) provides a short list of metric equivalents.

We hope you enjoy the following recipes.

Winter

January, Week 1

Crespelle (fresh manicotti)

Ingredients:
CRESPELLE

For the sauce	For the filling
Olive oil	*Ricotta*
Onion	*Whole beaten eggs*
Tomato (frozen or canned)	*Parmigiano*
Nutmeg	*Salt & white pepper*
White pepper	*Nutmeg*
Dried basil	

In the bleak mid-Winter, as the Christmas tree comes down and the candles dim, it's a good time to take out the last of the frozen summer tomatoes and make a fresh light sauce for CRESPELLE (or fresh manicotti). As luck would have it, this January morning saw Hawthorne Valley Farm selling farm-fresh ricotta. *The sauce:* chop 1 medium onion and sauté in olive oil until translucent, *but do not brown.* Add milled sea salt & white pepper, then add 2 cups chopped tomato, a few dustings of nutmeg and 3 or 4 crushed dried basil leaves. *The filling:* in a bowl mix 1 cup ricotta, 2 beaten eggs, nutmeg, salt, white pepper and about 2 tbsps. grated Parmigiano. Fill each flat crespella with about 1 tbsp. of the ricotta mixture and roll. Place in a baking dish that's been brushed with olive oil. Ladle the sauce over the CRESPELLE. Bake in a 350° F oven for about 20 minutes until lightly browned and heated through. Top with grated Parmigiano to taste.

January, Week 2

Fusilli with kale and smoked oysters

Ingredients:
Fusilli	*Kale*
Olive oil (extra vergine)	*Sea salt*
Pepperoncini	*Smoked oysters*
Garlic	

There's not much left in the market this time of year, and smoked oysters may not be to everyone's taste. Still, the crispness and fresh taste of the kale contrast well with the smoky, smooth texture of the oysters *(not from Union Square: 1 can left over from New Year's Day. You can also use smoked mussels.).* Heat the oil over moderate heat. Use 2 good-sized cloves of garlic: chop, slice, press or use whole. Sauté in the olive oil until translucent. *(Do not brown.)* Add 2 to 4 pepperoncini. Add 2 cups de-ribbed and chopped kale and the salt, turning the kale constantly until tender and coated with the oil and garlic. Add a little boiling water from the pasta pot from time to time. When the pasta is done, transfer to the sauté pan and stir into the sauce. Add the smoked oysters and turn the pasta gently so that the oysters do not fall apart. The pasta should glisten with oil, not water. Cover pan and bring to table.

January, Week 3

Fettuccine with smoked trout

Ingredients:

Fettuccine	*Cream*
Olive oil	*Dill*
Shallots	*Salt & white pepper*
Smoked trout	

Max Creek Hatchery smokes its trout over apple wood. Separate down the spine, carefully removing any remaining bones, then gently crumble into 2-inch pieces with a wooden fork. Heat the oil over moderate heat and add 2 finely chopped medium shallots and milled sea salt. Sauté until they turn translucent, *but do not brown*. When the pasta is done transfer to the sauté pan and stir into the oil and shallot. Then lower the heat, add 1 cup cream (at room temperature) and stir in. Add the crumbled smoked trout, ground white pepper and stir in. Garnish with chopped dill (fresh or freeze dried). Cover pan and bring to table.

January, Week 4

Spaghetti alla carbonara

Ingredients:

Spaghetti	*Salt & black pepper*
Olive oil	*Pecorino*
Guanciale	*Parsley (optional)*
Eggs	

The man from Flying Pigs Farm explained why they do not make either pancetta or guanciale: they smoke their pork, and these Italian meats are salt-brine cured: not an easy process for a small farm to win USDA approval. Only the eggs and pecorino are from the Market this time of year. The big carbonara questions? It originated in Naples, some time after World War II. We use guanciale not pancetta, and pecorino not Parmigiano.

While the spaghetti cooks, in a small frying pan heat the olive oil and add 1 heaping tbsp. finely chopped guanciale until it is translucent. Do not brown it. Meanwhile, in a large ceramic serving bowl beat 2 eggs well, add lots of black pepper milled coarse, a little sea salt and a ½ cup of grated pecorino. Beat well until fluffy. Just before the pasta is done, first gently add into the egg mixture the oil used to cook down the guanciale (this heats the eggs without cooking them). Continue to gently stir the mixture, then add the guanciale itself and stir in. Use a wooden pasta fork to lift the pasta from the boiling water into the same bowl. Stir in the pasta quickly. Throw in a small handful of finely chopped parsley, if you like. Bring the bowl to the table and serve immediately with wooden serving pieces.

January, Week 5

Rigatoni with roasted butternut squash

Ingredients:

Rigatoni	*Butternut squash*
Olive oil	*Salt*
Pepperoncini	*Sage leaves*
Butter	*Pecorino*

Peel, clean and cut 1 butternut squash into 2-inch cubes. Toss in 2 tbsp. softened butter and ½ tsp. pepperoncini flakes. Place on a flat baking pan and bake at about 375° F for 20 minutes, tossing once or twice, until the squash is nicely caramelized. Heat the oil in a sauté pan, add the caramelized squash, a little more butter and some salt. Add a little bit of boiling pasta water from time to time to keep moist. When the pasta is done, drain and add into the pan with 4 to 6 dried sage leaves and mix well. Cover pan and bring to table. Add pecorino to taste.

February, Week 1

Pasta e fagioli

Ingredients:

Brichetti	*Salt & white pepper*
Olive oil	DRIED WHITE BEANS
Garlic	*Dried basil*
Tomatoes	*Pecorino*

On Wednesdays throughout the year we can buy dried WHITE BEANS from Cayuga Pure Organic. While the Brichetti cook (about 10 minutes), heat the oil. Use 2 good-sized cloves of garlic: chop, slice, press or use whole. Sauté in the oil until translucent. *(Do not brown.)* Add 1 chopped tomato, salt & white pepper and sauté until the tomato is soft, adding a little water from the pasta pot from time to time. Add 1 pint cooked WHITE BEANS and stir in well. When the Brichetti are a little softer than *al dente,* add to the beans and sauce, stirring until any extra water is absorbed and the pasta glistens from the oil. Top with some crushed dried basil. Cover pan and bring to table. Sprinkle with grated pecorino, if desired. Romans like this dish a bit more soupy.

February, Week 2

Farfalle with pancetta and caramelized parsnip

Ingredients:

Farfalle	*Salt & black pepper*
Olive oil	*Pecorino*
Pancetta	*Cream*
Parsnip	*Parsley*
Leeks	

February is hard on vegetables. But in the market this week there are still some hardy winter types. Peal and cut 1 parsnip into 2-inch juliennes. Toss in melted butter, milled sea salt & white pepper. Place on a flat baking pan and bake at about 375° F for 20 minutes until nicely caramelized. Heat some oil in the sauté pan. Add 1 heaping tbsp. pancetta and sauté until translucent but not crisp. Add 1 cleaned, sliced and chopped leek (white part only), salt and ground black pepper and sauté until soft and translucent. Add the parsnip and stir, adding a bit of the pasta water. When the pasta is softer than *al dente,* drain and add to the pan, mixing into the sauce 1 cup of cream (at room temperature) and chopped parley. Heat through until the cream is absorbed by the pasta, but do not allow it to boil. Cover pan and bring to table.

February, Week 3

Bucatini with calamari

Ingredients:

Bucatini	*Tomato*
Olive oil	*Sea salt*
Pepperoncini	*Calamari*
Garlic	*Parsley*

P.E. & D.D. Seafood are back this week, and the calamari is fresh and cleaned. Take about ½ lb. calamari. Remove any inner bone, cut into rings and wash thoroughly, along with the tentacle tops. Heat the oil in the sauté pan along with 2 to 4 pepperoncini. Use 2 good-sized cloves of garlic: chop, slice, press or use whole. Sauté in the oil until translucent. *(Do not brown.)* Add 1 chopped tomato and just a little salt *(the calamari are salty),* and sauté until the tomato is soft, adding a little water from the pasta pot from time to time. Add the calamari, stirring constantly until well coated with the sauce. Cook this down for about 10 minutes. When the bucatini are just beyond *al dente,* add to the sauce, stirring until any extra water is absorbed and the pasta glistens from the oil. Stir in some chopped parsley. Cover pan and bring to table.

February, Week 4

Lumache with ceci and kale

Ingredients:

Lumache	CECI *(garbanzo beans, chick peas)*
Olive oil	**Kale*
Garlic	*Salt*
Pepperoncini	*Pecorino*

Kale still rules the Market. One farm stand also sells dried CECI, which they usually make into hummus. Heat the oil in the sauté pan along with 2 to 4 pepperoncini. Use 2 good-sized cloves of garlic: chop, slice, press or use whole. Sauté in the oil until translucent. *(Do not brown.)* Add about 1 lb. soaked and cooked CECI and stir in until well coated. De-rib and chop ½ lb. cleaned kale into small pieces, add salt and stir into the sauté pan until soft, adding a little water from the pasta pot from time to time. Add the lumache, stirring until any extra water is absorbed and the pasta glistens from the oil. Cover pan and bring to table. Serve with grated pecorino to taste.

* *If you want a more classic pasta ceci, omit the kale.*

March, Week 1

Spinach fettuccine with crimini

Ingredients:

Spinach fettuccine	*Salt*
Olive oil	*Crimini*
Pancetta	*Peas*
Garlic	*Pecorino*
Carrots	

Carrots are still with us, and the folks from Bulich Mushroom are back. We've picked their delicious crimini. Heat the oil in the sauté pan. Cut about 1 heaping tbsp. pancetta into tiny cubes and heat in the oil until translucent. Add 2 good-sized cloves of garlic sliced and sautéed in the oil until translucent. *(Do not brown.)* Grate 1 large carrot and add to the sauce, cooking until soft, adding a little salt and some water from the pasta pot from time to time. When the fettuccine are just *al dente,* add to the sauce. Add 1 cup defrosted peas, the cream (at room temperature) and about 2 tbsps. of pecorino. Stir all these into the fettuccine until all the water is absorbed and the pasta glisten with the oils. Cover pan and bring to table.

March, Week 2

Spaghetti aglio e olio with crimini

Ingredients:
Spaghetti	**Crimini*
Olive oil	*Sea salt*
Pepperoncini	*Savory*
Garlic	*Pecorino*

Spaghetti *aglio e olio* (with garlic and oil) is a time-honored standard in many parts of Italy. A nice *aglio olio* is so simple and good for whatever ails, from an upset stomach to a bad day at the office. It's often paired with thinly sliced mushrooms. Heat the oil in the sauté pan. Add 2 to 4 small pepperoncini whole or some flakes to taste. Then add 2 good-sized cloves of garlic sliced and sauté in the oil until translucent. *(Do not brown.)* Slice 8 to 12 crimini very thin, add to the oil, then add milled sea salt and sauté until well browned. Stir, adding a little water from the pasta pot from time to time. When the spaghetti are *al dente,* add to the sauce, stirring until any extra water is absorbed and the pasta glistens from the oil. Top with some crushed savory. Cover pan and bring to table. Top with pecorino to taste.

* *Omit the crimini if you want a more classic aglio e olio.*

March, Week 3

Spaghetti alla chitarra with walnuts

Ingredients:

Spaghetti alla chitarra	*Bread crumbs (rough)*
Extra vergine olive oil	*Walnuts*
Pepperoncini	*Sea salt*
Garlic	*Thyme*

Longer days keep promising things to come, but the stalls keep looking back to winter. We're using some of our dried baguette from Bread Alone. This dish is called *Spaghetti al fornaia*, or Baker's Spaghetti, because of the toasted bread crumbs. *Spaghetti alla chitarra* is fresh, soft spaghetti that is more absorbent. This is another very simple but satisfying winter dish with strong flavors, best served with a good, hardy red. Heat enough of the oil in the sauté pan. Add 2 to 4 small pepperoncini whole or in flakes to taste, then 2 or 3 good-sized cloves of garlic (chopped fine or pressed) and sauté in the oil until slightly brown. Add 1 cup rough-cut bread crumbs and sauté until brown. *Do not add any water from the pasta pot. Add more oil, instead.* Then add about 12 shelled walnuts, chopped small, and a little milled sea salt. When the spaghetti are *al dente,* add to the sauce, stirring until they glisten from the oil. Top with some thyme. Cover pan and bring to table.

March, Week 4

Rigatoni with Genovese sauce

Ingredients:

Rigatoni	Onion
Butter	Salt & white pepper
Celery	Dry white wine★
Carrots	Parmigiano
Short ribs (optional)★	

This recipe makes the best of the carrots and onions that are still at the Market. We've added short ribs from New York Beef Company.

★The recipe calls for cooking a 3-lb. beef eye-round roast with the vegetables. Those who want the flavor of the beef can braise 2 short ribs in ¼ lb. butter until well browned, removing them from the pot before de-glazing with a cup of white wine and then adding the finely chopped vegetables.

Take 4 medium carrots, 2 stalks celery, 2 lbs. onions, either together or one at a time (depending on your blender) and puree. Heat the butter in a high cast iron pot or dutch oven until clarified. Add the pureed vegetables, salt & milled white pepper. Add enough water *(★or 3 parts water and 1 white wine, if the meat has been used)* to double the level. (★Add the braised ribs back in.) Bring to a low boil, lower the heat and simmer, adding liquid as necessary. Cook down the vegetable mixture (and the meat) for 4–6 hours. The sauce should be thick, butter-creamy and not watery. *(★If you've used the short ribs, the meat should have come off the bones and been shredded fine with a wooden fork.)* When the rigatoni are done, drain well and transfer to a large ceramic bowl. Add enough of the sauce to coat the pasta well: it should glisten. Then top each dish served with a generous portion of the Genovese sauce and with lots of grated Parmigiano.

Spring

April, Week 1

Busiate with scallops and shiitake mushrooms

Ingredients:

Busiate	*Shallot*
Olive oil	*Salt & white pepper*
Butter	*Parsley*
Scallops	*Rosemary*
Pancetta	*Saffron*
Shiitake mushrooms	*Lemon zest*

We first had this dish in the early 1990s as a paella in Galicia on the way to Compostela. That recipe used serrano ham and oyster mushrooms instead of pancetta and shiitake. Place 2 dozen small bay scallops (or 6 large sea, quartered) in a bowl with a little sea salt and turn until salt is dissolved. In a separate pot make a stock from 1 cup of water, 1 small scallop chopped, 1 tsp. lemon zest, 1 tsp. finely chopped rosemary and a pinch of saffron. Bring to boil, cover and keep warm. Heat the oil in the pan over medium flame. Turn the scallops in the pan until they are coated with the oil and have turned white. Remove and cover. In the same oil, add a pat of butter and heat until clear. Chop about 6 two-inch-wide slices of pancetta and sauté until translucent. Next add about 6 large shiitake mushrooms, thinly sliced, ground sea salt and white pepper. Sauté until well browned and soft. Add 1 large chopped shallot and chopped parsley. Add some of the reserved stock to the sauté pan from time to time to keep the mixture moist. When the Busiate are just past *al dente* (about 12 minutes), drain and add to the pan, then add the reserved scallops and any remaining stock. Mix thoroughly until the sauce thickens and the pasta glistens with the oils. Cover pan and bring to table.

April, Week 2

Orecchiette with broccoli rabe

Ingredients:

Orecchiette	*Broccoli rabe*
Olive oil	*Salt*
Pepperoncini	*Pecorino*
Garlic	

The first broccoli rabe at the Market are "wintered over," that is, Bodhitree Farm plants very late in the fall, and the plants come up first thing in the spring. In case of frost they cover them, but the broccoli are farm-grown, outdoors. Rinse or soak about ½ lb. broccoli. Cut off the dried stem bottoms, remove some of the larger leaves, then chop stems, leaves and flower heads into small (2-inch) pieces. Parboil them in the pasta water for 1-2 minutes. Heat the oil in the sauté pan, add 2 to 4 pepperoncini. Use 2 good-sized cloves of garlic: chop, slice, press or use whole. Sauté in the oil until translucent. *(Do not brown.)* Remove the broccoli from the water with a slotted spoon, add to the pan with some salt and sauté until quite soft and creamy, adding a bit of the boiling pasta water from time to time. Drain the pasta and add to the pan. Stir until all the water is absorbed and the pasta glistens with the oil. Cover pan and bring to table. Top with pecorino to taste.

April, Week 3

Fettuccine with ramps and morels

Ingredients:

Fettuccine	*Salt & white pepper*
Olive oil	*Morels*
Butter	*Ramps*
Garlic	*Pecorino*

You have to get to the Market very early these days to beat the restaurant buyers to the ramps. Honey Hollow Farm provides the ramps and we add the morels from Whole Foods. Heat the oil and about ¼ cup butter in the sauté pan. Add 1 clove sliced garlic until translucent. *(Do not brown.)* Cut off the hard stem bottoms and cut 6-8 morels in half lengthwise. Add to the pan, stirring gently until coated with the butter and oil. Add salt and milled white pepper. Soak about ½ lb. of ramps until clean of any sand and dirt, remove the bottom portion of the stems. Parboil them in the pasta water for half a minute. Add to the pan, along with a bit of the boiling pasta water from time to time. Drain the cooked pasta and add to the pan, stirring it into the sauce until any extra water is absorbed and the pasta glistens with the oil and butter. Cover pan and bring to table. Top with pecorino to taste.

April, Week 4

Fettuccine with asparagus and shrimp

Ingredients:

Fettuccine	*Tomato*
Olive oil	*Sea salt & white pepper*
Pepperoncini	*Shrimp*
Garlic	*Asparagus*

The first ASPARAGUS have arrived at Cedar Hill Farm/Kernan Farms and will be in season for about the next month. The Greenmarket fish people do not catch shrimp this far north, but P.E. & D.D. Seafood does sometimes sell lobster, which you might substitute here. Heat the oil and 2-4 pepperoncini in the sauté pan. Use 2 good-sized cloves of garlic: chop, slice, press or use whole. Sauté in the oil until translucent. *(Do not brown.)* Add 1 chopped tomato along with sea salt and milled white pepper and sauté until soft. Add about 8 cleaned, medium shrimp (halved, butterflied or whole) and cook until pink. Meanwhile, clean about 12 thin ASPARAGUS of any hard scales and the woody bottom of stems and soak in water to remove any sand. Cut into 2-inch pieces, leaving the tips whole. Parboil in the pasta water for about 2 minutes. Remove with slotted spoon and add to the pan, stirring into the sauce until soft. When the pasta is done, drain and add to the pan, stirring into the sauce until any extra water is absorbed and the pasta glistens from the oil. Cover pan and bring to table.

May, Week 1

Vesuvio with fiddleheads

Ingredients:

Vesuvio	*Spring garlic*
Olive oil	*Salt & white pepper*
Butter	*Fiddleheads*
Pancetta	*Pecorino*

Still early enough to catch the fiddleheads, now at Berried Treasures. We used Vesuvio (little swirls like the gases that steam from the volcano) because they match the fiddlehead shape so perfectly. Rinse and soak ½ lb. of fiddleheads thoroughly, changing the water once or twice to get out the brown dried leaves and any sand or dirt. Boil them in a separate pot until you can pierce with a fork. Meanwhile, add the oil and butter to a sauté pan and sauté about 1 heaping tbsp. pancetta until translucent. Clean and chop fine about 6 small heads of spring garlic fine and add to the pan with some salt and milled white pepper, sautéing until soft. Then add in boiled fiddleheads. Add a bit of the boiling pasta water from time to time. Drain the cooked pasta and add to the pan, stirring it into the sauce until any extra water is absorbed and the pasta glistens with the oil and butter. Cover pan and bring to table. Top with pecorino to taste.

May, Week 2

Penne with creamed asparagus

Ingredients:

Penne	*Salt & white pepper*
Olive oil	*Cream*
Butter	*Parsley*
ASPARAGUS	*Pecorino*

Use about ½ lb. of the fatter ASPARAGUS for this and clean.
Pressure cook or boil until soft. Place in blender with some of
cooking water until creamy. Meanwhile heat the oil and about
¼ cup butter in the sauté pan. Add the creamed asparagus, salt
and milled white pepper, cooking over medium to low heat until
most of water cooks away. Drain and add the cooked penne,
combining with 1 cup cream (at room temperature). When thoroughly mixed and heated, top with a little chopped parley. Cover
pan and bring to table. Top with grated pecorino to taste.

May, Week 3

Fettuccine with spinach, Sicilian style

Ingredients:

Fettuccine	*Anchovy fillets*
Olive oil	*Spinach*
Pepperoncini	*Sultanas*
Garlic	*Pine nuts (pinoli)*

Spinach is still going strong at Bodhitree Farm. Trim ½ lb. of fresh spinach of any stems and brown on the leaves and soak well to remove any sand and dirt, changing the water as necessary. Spin dry and chop. Heat the oil in the sauté pan, add 2-4 pepperoncini. Use 2 good-sized cloves of garlic: chop, slice, press or use whole. Sauté in the oil until translucent. *(Do not brown.)* Add 1 or 2 anchovy fillets with some of their oil and stir in until dissolved. Add the chopped spinach and sauté down until soft. Add about ½ cup sultanas and ¼ cup pine nuts, using a bit of the boiling pasta water from time to time to keep the sauce moist. Drain the cooked pasta and add to the pan, stirring it into the sauce until any extra water is absorbed and the pasta glistens from the oil. Cover pan and bring to table.

May, Week 4

Ravioli with asparagus and mushrooms

Ingredients:

Ravioli (cheese)	*Spring onion*
Olive oil	*ASPARAGUS*
Pancetta	*Shell peas*
White-cap mushrooms	*Cream*
Salt & white pepper	*Pecorino*

ASPARAGUS are still holding on, while Cedar Hill Farm/Kernan Farms from far southern New Jersey have brought the first of the spring shell peas. Chop and sauté 1 heaping tbsp. pancetta in the olive oil until translucent. Section ½ lb. of mushrooms into eights and add to the oil and pancetta. Add salt and ground white pepper, sautéing over medium-high heat until golden brown. Lower the heat and sauté 1 chopped spring onion until soft. Meanwhile, clean the ASPARAGUS, cut them into 2 inch lengths (leaving the tips whole), and parboil them for about 2 minutes in the pasta water. Remove and add to the sauce. Shell about ½ lb. of peas and parboil in the same water for about 2 minutes. Remove and add to the pan. Add a bit of the boiling pasta water from time to time to keep the sauce moist. Drop the ravioli into boiling water to which you've added a few drops of olive oil. When the ravioli are done, transfer gently into the sauce. Add 1 cup cream (at room temperature) and fold all together gently until heated through, *but do not allow the cream to boil.* Cover pan and bring to table. Top with grated pecorino to taste.

June, Week 1

Strozzapreti with CHARD and fresh ricotta

Ingredients:

Strozzapreti	*Salt*
Extra vergine oil	CHARD
Pepperoncini	*Fresh ricotta*
Shallots	*Pecorino*

Hawthorne Valley Farm, Dancing Ewe Farm, and Valley Shepherd Creamery now produce fresh ricotta, ricotta salata, mozzarella or smoked mozzarella. Heat the oil in the sauté pan, add 2-4 pepperoncini. Chop 2 medium shallots and add to the oil, add salt and sauté until translucent. Add about 2 cups cooked CHARD, using a bit of the boiling pasta water from time to time to keep the sauce moist. When the pasta is cooked softer than *al dente,* add to the pan. Then stir in 1 cup ricotta over low heat until warmed through, any water is absorbed and the pasta glistens. Cover pan and bring to table. Top with grated pecorino to taste.

June, Week 2

Spaghetti with zucchini and milk

Ingredients:

Spaghetti	*Salt & pepper*
Olive oil	*★Milk*
Garlic	*Dried Basil*
Green & yellow zucchini	*Pecorino*

Zucchini are now all over the Market. The key to this recipe is the contrast between the tangy squash and the cream. Clean and quarter 2 zucchini lengthwise, then slice into 1-inch sections. Heat the oil in the sauté pan. Slice 2 good-sized cloves of garlic and sauté in the oil until slightly browned. Add the zucchini, salt and ground white pepper and sauté until lightly caramelized. Add ½ cup of ★milk and cook over medium heat until it almost starts to form a custard (15–20 minutes). Drain the cooked pasta and add to the pan, stirring it into the sauce until any extra water is absorbed and the pasta glistens from the oil and milk. Top with crushed, dried basil. Cover pan and bring to table. Add grated pecorino to taste.

★You can substitute half-and-half for the milk.

June, Week 3

Pasta piselli

Ingredients:

Ditalini	*Salt & white pepper*
Olive oil	*Shell peas*
Pancetta	*Pecorino*
Spring onion	

Heaps of fresh shell peas now at the stands call for *pasta piselli*.
Heat the oil in the sauté pan. Add 1-2 tbsps. chopped pancetta
and heat until translucent, but do not brown. Add 2 chopped
spring onions, salt and milled white pepper and sauté until soft.
Shell 1 cup peas and parboil in the pasta water for 1-2 minutes.
Transfer them to the pan and heat for about 5 minutes. Add a
bit of the boiling pasta water from time to time to keep the sauce
moist. When the pasta are done, add a ladle of the pasta water to
the pan, drain the pasta and transfer to the pan. Cook down over
medium heat, stirring until the pasta glistens and all the water
has been absorbed. Cover pan and bring to table. Top with grated
pecorino to taste.

June, Week 4

Fettuccine with fava, peas and zucchini

Ingredients:

Fettuccine	*Salt & white pepper*
Olive oil	*Fava beans*
Pancetta	*Shell peas*
Spring onion	*Pecorino*
Zucchini	

FAVA are the big new thing now at Phillips Farms, Berried Treasures and Bodhitree Farm. Prepare about 1 lb. unshelled FAVA. Shell and parboil about 1 cup peas for 1-2 minutes. Heat the oil and add about 1-2 tbsps. chopped pancetta. Sauté until it is translucent. Cut 2 zucchini into ½-inch cubes and add to pan with salt and milled white pepper and sauté for about 5 minutes. Add 2 finely chopped spring onions and sauté until soft, using a bit of the boiling pasta water from time to time to keep the sauce moist. Add the shelled FAVA and then the peas, stirring into the sauce, adding more water to keep the mixture moist while it softens. When the pasta is done, drain and add to the pan, stirring until any extra water is absorbed and the pasta glistens from the oil. Cover pan and bring to table. Top with grated pecorino to taste.

Summer

July, Week 1

Penne all'arrabbiata

Ingredients:

Penne	*Garlic*
Olive oil	*Tomato*
Pepperoncini	*Salt*
Pancetta	*Parsley*

Tomatoes have arrived! We like the balance of heirloom, beef-steak, cherries and other varieties best at S & S.O. Produce, though later in the year we also buy them in bulk at Van Houten Farms. *Penne arrabbiata* (raging pens) always bring back the memory of a hot summer afternoon, sitting outside a small trattoria opposite the Cancelleria in Rome, marvelling at the hot, tangy *penne*, done just this side of *al dente.* This is a simple dish to make, as long as you're not afraid of garlic, oil and *heat.* Heat the oil in the sauté pan. Add about 6 pepperoncini and stir. Add in 2 tbsps. chopped pancetta and heat until translucent. Add 3 cloves of garlic, sliced thin, and sauté until translucent, *but do not brown.* Add 2 cups chopped fresh tomato and salt. Sauté over high heat, using a bit of the boiling pasta water from time to time to keep the sauce moist. When the penne are *al dente,* drain and add to the pan, stirring until any extra water is absorbed and the pasta glistens from the oils. Stir in the chopped parsley. Cover pan and bring to table. *Do not use grated cheese.*

July, Week 2

Fettuccine with pesto and potato

Ingredients:

Fettuccine	*Sea Salt*
Olive oil	*Parmigiano*
PESTO	*New potatoes*

Basil is everywhere at the Market, but we buy from Tamarack Hollow Farm when we want smaller, clean bunches. We avoid ones with flowered stems: they tend to be more bitter. Make your PESTO. Cut 4 small new potatoes into ½ to 1-inch cubes and boil for 1 minute in the pasta water, to which you've added some olive oil. Then add the fettuccine and cook for another 3-4 minutes. Meanwhile, in the sauté pan, heat enough olive oil over low heat and add 2-3 tbsps. of the PESTO. Drain the pasta and potatoes and add to pan. Mix well. Cover pan and bring to table. Top each serving with extra PESTO, cheese and even a little more olive oil to taste.

July, Week 3

Fregola with carciofini and calamaretti

Ingredients:

Fregola	*Salt & black pepper*
Olive oil	*Small calamari*
Garlic	*Baby* ARTICHOKES
Tomato	

Baby ARTICHOKES have been appearing at the Market at the
S&SO Produce stand for about 10 years: they are now tender,
green and full of flavor. We first had this recipe with *fregola* (an
Italian couscous) in a small restaurant on the south coast of
Sardinia near the ancient ruins at Nora. The *fregola* we used here
are large and have a toasted finish. They take about 15 minutes to
cook through.

Clean about 4 ARTICHOKES, cut into eighths, and in a separate pot
boil the sections for about 10 minutes or until you can pierce
easily with a fork. Meanwhile, use 2 good-sized cloves of garlic:
chop, slice, press or use whole. Sauté in the oil until translucent. *(Do
not brown.)* Add 1 cup chopped tomato, a little milled sea salt *(the
calamari are salty)* and milled black pepper and cook down. Clean
about ½ lb. calamari, cut the body into rings, leave the tentacles
whole and add it all to the sauce. Cook for 5–10 minutes, using
a bit of the boiling pasta water from time to time to keep moist.
Add the boiled artichoke sections. Mix the sauce well and add
the cooked and drained *fregola*. Stir in over moderate heat until
warmed through, any water is absorbed, and the pasta glistens
with the oil. Cover pan and bring to table.

July, Week 4

Risotto al fior' di zucca (ZUCCHINI BLOSSOMS)

Ingredients:

Arborio rice	*VEGETABLE STOCK*
Butter	*Saffron*
Pancetta	*ZUCCHINI BLOSSOMS*
Spring onion	*Parmigiano*
Salt & white pepper	

So this isn't pasta, but now at least three stands are selling
ZUCCHINI BLOSSOMS at reasonable prices. We usually buy from
Windfall Farms. This is one of the best ways to serve these blossoms. Boil just over 2 cups of the VEGETABLE STOCK in a separate
pot. Melt about ¼ cup butter in the sauté pan over moderate
heat and add 1-2 tbsps. chopped pancetta. Sauté until translucent
but not browned. Add 2 chopped spring onions, salt and ground
white pepper and sauté until soft. Stir in 1 cup arborio rice and
turn in the mixture until all the rice is coated and glistens. Then
lower the heat and add the first cup of VEGETABLE STOCK and
the crushed saffron, stirring it in but allowing the rice to slowly
bubble undisturbed until the stock is absorbed. Keep adding
more stock until the rice is cooked through. When done, add in
6 large cleaned and sliced ZUCCHINI BLOSSOMS, turn off the heat,
stir gently until the blossoms wilt. Cover pan and bring to table.
Top with grated Parmigiano to taste.

July, Week 5

Vesuvio with zucchini and shrimp

Ingredients:

Vesuvio	*Zucchini*
Olive oil	*Sea salt*
Pepperoncini	*Shrimp*
Garlic	

This is a dish that we first had on a cliff side at Castellammare di Stabia on the Sorrentine Peninsula, looking back toward Naples and Mt. Vesuvius, so the pasta is just right. Heat the oil over high heat and add 2-4 pepperoncini. Lower the heat and add 2 good-sized cloves of garlic: chop, slice, press or use whole. Sauté in the oil until translucent. *(Do not brown.)* Clean and cut 2 medium zucchini into 1-inch cubes and add to the sauce with some milled sea salt, using a bit of the boiling pasta water from time to time until the zucchini are quite soft and creamy. Add about 8 medium cleaned shrimp either in sections or butterflied. Turn in the sauce until pink. Drain the pasta and add to the pan, stirring over high heat until any water is absorbed and the pasta glistens from the oil. Cover pan and bring to table.

August, Week 1

Fettuccine with carciofini

Ingredients:

Fettuccine	*Salt & white pepper*
Olive oil	*Baby ARTICHOKES*
Pancetta	*Cream*
Garlic	*Pecorino*
Spring onion	

ARTICHOKES now have a long season at S&SO Produce. We bought the greenest and smallest we could find. Clean and section about 6 ARTICHOKES into eighths and boil in the pasta water for 5–10 minutes. Sauté 1 heaping tbsp. chopped pancetta in the olive oil until translucent. Add 2 cloves of garlic sliced into thirds lengthwise and sauté until soft. *(But do not brown.)* Chop 1 spring onion and add to the pan with some salt and ground white pepper. Sauté until soft, using a bit of the boiling pasta water from time to time to keep the sauce moist. Add the boiled ARTICHOKE sections, gently stirring into the sauce. When the fettuccine are done, drain and add to the sauce, then add 1 cup cream (at room temperature). Gently mix until warmed through, but do not allow the cream to boil. Cover pan and bring to table. Top with grated pecorino to taste.

August, Week 2

Ziti rigati with RATATOUILLE

Ingredients:
  Ziti rigati
  RATATOUILLE
  Grated pecorino

This is always the season for Provençal RATATOUILLE. Everything
is available at the general stands like Cedar Hill Farm/Kernan
Farms, Migliorelli Farm, S & S.O. Produce: eggplant, zucchini,
tomato, garlic, green peppers, onion. We usually make it and let
it stand overnight, then have it the first day with BEANS, oil, sage
and a good baguette. As the supply goes down, we will use some
with rigatoni or ziti. Heat about 2 cups in the sauté pan, using a
bit of the boiling pasta water from time to time to keep the sauce
moist. When the pasta is done, add to the pan and stir, making
sure any water is absorbed and the pasta glistens with the sauce.
Cover pan and bring to table. Top with grated pecorino to taste.

August, Week 3

Bucatini alla puttanesca

Ingredients:

Bucatini	*Tomato*
Olive oil	*Capers*
Pepperoncini	*Gaeta olives*
Garlic	*Parsley*
Anchovy fillets	

Murray's Cheese shop is not at the Market, but it's on Bleecker Street, only an extra ten-minute walk, where we get some very good anchovies, olives and capers. This is a sauce that becomes thick and savory from the mixture of these ingredients. Heat 2-4 pepperoncini in the oil. Use 2 good-sized cloves of garlic: chop, slice, press or use whole. Sauté in the oil until translucent. *(Do not brown.)* Add about 4 anchovy fillets and stir in until they dissolve in the oil. Add 1 large, chopped tomato, about 20 capers and about 12 Gaeta olives, pitted and cut in half. Add a bit of the boiling pasta water from time to time to keep the sauce moist. When the pasta is done, add to the pan and stir, making sure any water is absorbed and the pasta glistens with the oils. Mix in some finely chopped parsley at the last moment. Cover pan and bring to table.

August, Week 4

Spinach fettuccine al fior' di zucca (ZUCCHINI BLOSSOMS)

Ingredients:

Spinach Fettuccine	*Salt & pepper*
Olive oil	*ZUCCHINI BLOSSOMS*
Pancetta	*Pecorino*
White onion	

Heat 1 tbsp. chopped pancetta in the olive oil until translucent. *Do not brown.* Add 1 chopped small white onion, salt and ground white or black pepper and sauté until soft. Use a bit of the boiling pasta water from time to time to keep the sauce moist. Prepare about 6 large ZUCCHINI BLOSSOMS and slice crosswise into 2-inch sections. Drain the cooked fettuccine and add to the pan, then add the ZUCCHINI BLOSSOMS and gently turn in until the blossoms wilt. Add about ¼ cup of grated pecorino and stir in until the water has been absorbed and the pasta glistens from the oil and cheese. Cover pan and bring to table.

August, Week 5

Busiate with oyster mushrooms and ricotta

Ingredients:

Busiate	*Shallot*
Olive oil	*Sage leaves*
Butter	*Ricotta*
Oyster mushrooms	*Pecorino*
Salt & white pepper	

A few stands now sell oyster mushrooms, but we like Bulich Mushroom's. Peel the heads of the oyster mushrooms into separate trumpets, dividing the larger trumpets in half lengthwise. Remove the tough bottom stems. Heat the oil and 1 tbsp. butter in the sauté pan until the butter clarifies but does not brown. Add the oyster mushrooms, sea salt and milled white pepper and sauté over medium-high heat until well browned but not crisp. Lower the heat and add 1 finely chopped shallot and about 4 medium sage leaves chopped. Cover, adding a bit of the boiling pasta water from time to time to keep the sauce moist. When the busiate are just beyond *al dente* (about 12 minutes), reserve about 1 cup of the pasta water and add the busiate to the pan. Add 1 cup fresh ricotta and stir in. Then add about ¼ cup grated pecorino and stir in. Use some of the reserved pasta water to loosen the sauce if the ricotta binds the pasta too much. Garnish with a few reserved whole sage leaves. Cover pan and bring to table.

September, Week 1

Fettuccine with salsa fresca

Ingredients:

Fettuccine	Salt & pepper
Olive Oil	Grated Parmigiano
Onion	Basil leaves
Tomato	

Now that September is here, tomatoes are large, ripe and abundant. We still like S & S.O. Produce and Van Houten Farms. Salsa fresca is a most simple Neapolitan tomato sauce that depends on the freshest ingredients to make it work. Chop fine 1 small white onion. Sauté in the olive oil until translucent. Add 2 cups chopped tomato. Sprinkle with salt & pepper (white or black). Cover. Cook over medium high heat until the tomato breaks down. *Do not brown any of the onion or tomato.* Add a little boiling water from the pasta pot from time to time to keep the sauce moist. When the pasta is done, transfer to the sauté pan and stir into the sauce until any water is absorbed and the pasta glistens from the oil. Toss in a few chopped basil leaves. Cover pan and bring to table. For those who like, sprinkle grated Parmigiano to taste.

September, Week 2

Pasta alla Norma

Ingredients:

Fettuccine	Salt & black pepper
Olive oil	Tomato
Garlic	Basil leaves
Eggplant	Pecorino

Use 2 good-sized cloves of garlic: chop, slice, press or use whole.
Sauté in the olive oil until translucent. *(Do not brown.)* Buy the
smallest eggplants you can find: about 4 inches long. Bodhitree
Farm sells a good variety of small white, purple and speckled.
Cut about 6 in half lengthwise, and add to the garlic and oil
along with some salt and ground black pepper. Sauté until soft,
adding a little bit of the boiling pasta water to keep moist. Add
2 small chopped tomatoes. Sprinkle with salt & pepper. Cover.
Sauté over medium-high heat until the tomato breaks down.
When the fettuccine are done, transfer to the sauté pan and stir
into the sauce until any water is absorbed and the pasta glistens
from the oil. Toss in a few chopped basil leaves. Cover pan and
bring to table. Top with grated pecorino to taste.

September, Week 3

Conchiglie with peppers and tomato

Ingredients:

Conchiglie	*Peppers, green & red*
Olive oil	*Sea salt & white pepper*
Garlic	*Basil leaves*
Tomatoes, red & golden	

Conchiglie (sea shells) are perfect for this unheated dish that takes advantage of late summer vegetables. In a large ceramic serving bowl add 2-3 cloves of pressed garlic to a good amount of fresh, light olive oil and stir in well. Slice about 2 large tomatoes as thin as possible and cut 2 peppers into very thin slices and then into sections about 3 inches long. Add to the oil and garlic along with milled sea salt and white pepper. Mix thoroughly and let stand covered *but not refrigerated* for about 4 hours. Stir occasionally. Cook the pasta, drain and add to the bowl, mixing thoroughly until all the shells are coated with the sauce. Add some chopped basil or small basil leaves and bring to table either by the dish or in the bowl.

Note: some recipes for this dish call for chopped mozzarella or grated Parmigiano, but — if you want to add something — we think the fresh summer tastes of these vegetables come through best with fresh ricotta.

September, Week 4

Calamarata with zucchini and scamorza

Ingredients:

Calamarata	*Salt & pepper*
Olive oil	*Spring onions*
Garlic	*Tomato*
Green & yellow zucchini	*Scamorza (or smoked mozzarella)*

Calamarata takes its name from the rings of cut squid — calamari — that often accompanies this pasta. Heat the oil on medium flame. Use 2 good-sized cloves of garlic: chop, slice, press or use whole. Sauté in the oil until translucent. *(Do not brown.)* Cube about 1 small yellow and 2 small green zucchini and add to the sauce. Add the salt & pepper. The yellow will soften before the green. Add 1 small white or yellow onion and sauté in the olive oil until translucent. *(Do not brown.)* Then add 1 large chopped tomato. Use a little boiling water from the pasta pot from time to time to keep the sauce moist. The pasta is done when it begins to soften beyond *al dente* but still keeps its shape (12 or more minutes). Transfer it to the sauté pan and stir into the sauce. When the pasta begins to glisten from the oil, add about half a small scamorza cut into cubes or narrow strips. Lower the heat and continue to stir until the cheese has softened. Cover pan and bring to the table.

Autumn

October, Week 1

Vesuvio with Tuscan kale and (vegan) sausage

Ingredients:

Vesuvio	*Sausage (vegan or pork)*
Olive oil	*Kale*
Pepperoncini flakes	*Salt*
Garlic	*Grana padano*

The main idea behind the sausage is the fennel, hot pepper and texture against the slight bite of the kale, so either vegan or pork will work well. Clean, soak and drain about ½ lb. kale. Heat some pepperoncini flakes in the oil. Place 2 sausages in frying pan, cover with water and boil down all the liquid. Then brown them well in their own fat, or simply brown the vegan sausage in oil. Cut the sausages into sections and stir them into the sauté pan. Use 2 good-sized cloves of garlic: chop, slice, press or use whole. Sauté in the oil until translucent. *(Do not brown.)* Remove the ribs from the kale, slice the half-leaves into 1-inch ribbons, then add them to the pan along with some salt. Use a bit of the boiling pasta water from time to time to keep the sauce moist until the kale is soft. When the pasta is done, drain and add to the pan and stir, making sure any water is absorbed and the pasta glistens with the oils. Cover pan and bring to table. Top with grated grana padano to taste.

October, Week 2

Paglia e fieno with crimini and peas

Ingredients:

Paglia e fieno	*Salt & black pepper*
Olive oil	*Shallot*
Guanciale	*Summer (frozen) peas*
Garlic	*Pecorino*
Crimini mushrooms	

Paglia e fieno refers to the straw and hay colors of the yellow and green fettuccine, both sold at Knoll Krest Farm. As autumn comes in, it's good to remember high summer and time to use the peas you froze in August. Heat the oil in the pan over medium-high heat. Chop about 1 tbsp. guanciale and sauté until translucent but not brown. Use 2 good-sized cloves of garlic: chop, slice, press or use whole. Sauté in the oil until translucent. *(Do not brown.)* Cut about 12 crimini into eighths and add to the pan over high heat, along with some salt and ground black pepper, sautéing until deep brown but not crisp. Lower the heat. Chop 1 large shallot and add to the sauté pan. Use a bit of the boiling pasta water from time to time to keep the sauce moist. Parboil about 1 cup peas for 1-2 minutes in the pasta water, then remove and add to the sauce. When the pasta is done, drain and add to the pan and stir, making sure any water is absorbed and the pasta glistens with the oils. Cover pan and bring to table. Top with grated pecorino to taste.

October, Week 3

Pasta al forno

Ingredients:

MIXED PASTA
Olive oil
Garlic
Crimini mushrooms
Sausage (vegan, pork or lamb)
Escarole
Radicchio

Ricotta (1 pint)
Gorgonzola (mountain)
Fontina
Salt & white pepper
Sage leaves
Cream
Pecorino

Section about 12 crimini into eighths and sauté in oil with 3 cloves of sliced garlic until the mushrooms are deep brown. Set aside. Boil down 2 pork or lamb sausages until cooked and brown well in the remaining fat or oil; or brown 2 vegan sausages in oil. Cut the sausages into sections and set aside. Soak, rinse, drain and chop ½ head of radicchio and ½ head of escarole. Meanwhile, cut ¼ lb. Gorgonzola and ¼ lb. Fontina into small cubes and set aside. In a very large pot boil 1 lb. of the MIXED PASTA for about 10 minutes or until the hardest shapes are soft. Drain well. In the same or another very large pot or bowl add the pasta. Then keep adding rounds of the ricotta, sausage, crimini, cheeses, radicchio and escarole, mixing very well. Add salt and ground white pepper to taste. Pour out the mixture into a large, oiled ceramic baking dish. Pour in 1½ cups cream, sprinkle well with grated pecorino and top with a few fresh sage leaves. Bake in a 425° F oven for about 20 minutes or until the pasta in well browned and crisp on top but still moist beneath. Let stand for 5–10 minutes. Bring to table in baking dish.

October, Week 4

Farfalle with broccoli

Ingredients:

Farfalle	*Broccoli*
Olive oil	*Salt*
Pepperoncini	*Pecorino*
Garlic	

We're almost at the end of the broccoli season, and much of it is best used well cooked. Clean and steam ½ lb. broccoli until tender but still firm. Drain and cut into small pieces. Heat 2-4 pepperoncini in the oil over high heat. Lower the heat and add 2 good-sized cloves of garlic: chop, slice, press or use whole. Sauté the garlic in the oil until translucent. *(Do not brown.)* Next, add the broccoli to the sauté pan along with some salt. Use a bit of the boiling pasta water from time to time to keep the sauce moist until the broccoli is very soft and forms a firm green sauce. When the pasta is done, drain, add to the pan and stir, making sure any water is absorbed and the pasta glistens with the oils. Cover pan and bring to table. Top with grated pecorino to taste.

October, Week 5

Bucatini with tuna, Sicilian style

Ingredients:

Bucatini	*Sea salt*
Olive oil	*Pine nuts*
Pepperoncini	*★Capers*
Tuna (steak or jarred)	*Sultanas or golden raisins*
Garlic	*Parsley*
Chopped tomato	

Blue Moon Fish sells high-quality tuna steak, swordfish and many other varieties of fish and shellfish. Use either about 6 ounces of a fresh tuna steak or 1 jar of good-quality preserved tuna (Ortiz, Calabrian Callipo, etc.). If using fresh tuna steak add a little more oil than usual. Cut the steak into thin (¼ to ½ inch) slices and add to the oil over medium-high heat until the tuna is well browned but not crisp. Lower the heat and add 2 pepperoncini and 2 cloves of garlic sliced thin. Sauté until the garlic is translucent. *(But do not brown.)* Add 2 cups of chopped tomato and sea salt and cook down until the sauce thickens. The tuna will begin to flake as you gently stir the sauce. Then add 1 heaping tbsp. of pine nuts, ½ cup sultanas or golden raisins and ¼ cup of ★capers. Use a bit of the boiling pasta water from time to time to keep the sauce moist. When the bucatini are done, add to the pan along with a handful of chopped parley and stir, making sure any water is absorbed and the pasta glistens with the oils. Cover pan and bring to table.

★If the capers are packed in salt, rinse thoroughly before adding to the sauce.

November, Week 1

Spaghetti alle vongole

Ingredients:
- *Spaghetti*
- *Olive oil*
- *Pepperoncini*
- *Sea salt*
- *Garlic*
- *Cockles or other small clams*
- *Parsley*

It's common knowledge that we have made this dish every Friday night for over 40 years. By now we think we have it right, and we've confirmed this recipe in many restaurants in Naples over the years. They use no butter, wine, vermouth, chicken stock, basil or anything else. The secret is the heated oil, sea salt and the calcium of the clam shells: they thicken to a glistening, creamy sauce. Real *vongole* are almost impossible to get here, even in New York. Use about 12 per person of the smallest little necks, cockles or Manila clams. Wash and rinse the clams in a large bowl for several hours until they have given up any sand, changing the water as needed. Heat 2-4 pepperoncini whole or in flakes in the hot oil. Add 2 good-sized cloves of garlic: chop, slice, press or use whole. Sauté the garlic in the oil until translucent. *(Do not brown.)* Add the clams in their shells and sprinkle with sea salt. Cover the pan. The clams will give off their stored liquid as they open, but use a bit of the boiling pasta water from time to time if the liquid starts to evaporate. Add the cooked and drained spaghetti and cook down the liquid over high heat until all the water is absorbed and the pasta glistens with the oil. Sprinkle with chopped parsley and stir in. Cover pan and bring to table.

November, Week 2

Penne with caramelized cabbage

Ingredients:

Penne	*Cabbage*
Olive oil	*Anchovy fillets*
Pepperoncini	*Bread crumbs*
Garlic	

This is a Mark Bittman recipe from the *New York Times* with some of our changes. Heat 2-4 pepperoncini in oil over high heat. Clean and shred ¼ head of cabbage into thin strips. Add to the oil and sauté over high heat, stirring constantly until the cabbage is well caramelized. Add 2 good-sized cloves of garlic: chop, slice, press or use whole. Sauté in the oil until translucent. *(Do not brown.)* Add about 4 anchovy fillets and stir until they dissolve into the sauce. Cover and use a bit of the boiling pasta water from time to time to keep the mixture moist. When the pasta is done, drain and add to the pan, stir in over high heat, then add about 2–3 tbsps. bread crumbs and stir until any water is absorbed and the pasta glistens with the oils. Cover pan and bring to table.

November, Week 3

Spaghetti alla chitarra with calamari and SALSA ANCONETANA

Ingredients:

Spaghetti alla chitarra	*Pepperoncini*
Olive oil	SALSA ANCONETANA
Calamari	*Parsley*

This is a dish that came to us after making baked *stoccafisso all'Anconetana* (salt cod, Ancona style). We used calamari and the sauce remaining from the baked salt cod. Clean and slice about ½ lb. calamari and then sauté them in the olive oil until cooked through but not browned. Add 2-4 pepperoncini to taste. *(The dried cod should provide all the salt to this dish that's needed.)* Then add the reserved SALSA ANCONETANA and cook down until the calamari are tender, adding some of the boiling pasta water as needed. When the spaghetti are cooked, drain well and add to the pan with some finely chopped parley. Stir in the pasta until all the extra liquid is absorbed and the pasta glistens from the oil. Cover pan and bring to table.

November, Week 4

Strozzapreti with cauliflower

Ingredients:

Strozzapreti	Cauliflower
Olive oil	Capers
Pepperoncini	Olive paste
Garlic	Parsley
Anchovy fillets	Pecorino

Cauliflower stands up well as we head toward Winter. Heat 2-4 pepperoncini in oil over high heat. Add 2 good-sized cloves of garlic: chop, slice, press or use whole. Sauté in the oil until translucent. *(Do not brown.)* Add 2-4 anchovy fillets and dissolve in the sauce. Cut or snap ½ a cauliflower into very small florets and parboil in the pasta water for about 5 minutes. Remove and stir into the sauté pan. Add about 2 dozen capers and then 1-2 tbsps. olive paste, stirring the sauce and adding some of the boiling pasta water until the cauliflower has softened into a consistent sauce. When the strozzapreti are soft just beyond *al dente*, drain and transfer to the pan, adding the chopped parsley and stirring over high heat until all the extra liquid is absorbed and the pasta glistens from the oil. Cover pan and bring to table. Top with grated pecorino to taste.

December, Week 1

Rigatoni with cabbage and crimini

Ingredients:

Rigatoni	*Crimini mushrooms*
Olive oil	*Salt*
Pepperoncini flakes	*Cabbage*
Guanciale	*Peas*
Garlic	*Pecorino*

Heat 1 tbsp. pepperoncini flakes in oil over medium heat. Add ¼ cup chopped guanciale and sauté until translucent, but not browned. Then add 2 good-sized cloves of garlic: chop, slice, press or use whole. Sauté in the oil until translucent. *(Do not brown.)* Cut about 12 crimini into eighths and add to the pan along with some salt, sautéing until golden. Raise the heat and add ¼ of a cabbage chopped, sautéing until soft, using a bit of the boiling pasta water from time to time to keep the mixture moist. Meanwhile, in a separate pan, parboil 1 cup peas for 1-2 minutes, drain and add to the sauce. When the pasta is just softer than *al dente,* drain and add to the pan, stirring until the sauce is absorbed and the pasta glistens with the oils. Cover pan and bring to table. Top with grated pecorino to taste.

December, Week 2

Spaghetti ai frutti di mare

Ingredients:

Spaghetti	Saffron
Olive oil	Calamari
Garlic	Clams (little neck)
Tomato	Mussels
Sea salt & white pepper	Parsley

Blue Moon Fish stays at the Market until December. This recipe uses much of what's still being offered. You'll need two large sauté pans: one for the sauce and all the shellfish, the other to mix the cooked spaghetti into the sauce and then add the seafood. Heat the oil over high heat. Add 2 good-sized cloves of garlic: chop, slice, press or use whole. Sauté in the oil until translucent. *(Do not brown.)* Add 2 cups chopped tomato, sea salt and ground white pepper, a pinch of saffron and cook down for about 3 minutes. Add ⅓ lb. cleaned calamari sliced into rings (leaving any tentacles whole), stirring constantly until the squid has begun to absorb the sauce. Next add 12 clams, and then 12 mussels. Stir into the sauce until coated. Cover the pan and raise the heat to medium until the shellfish open and release their liquid. Uncover and continue to reduce the liquid until the sauce thickens. When the pasta is done, take two ladles of the sauce and add it to the second pan. Drain the pasta and add to second pan, stirring over high heat until the sauce has been absorbed. Then add all the seafood, the remaining sauce from the first pan and the chopped parsley, stirring until the sauce is absorbed and the pasta glistens with the oil. Cover pan and bring to table.

December, Week 3

Paccheri with swordfish

Ingredients:

Paccheri	*★Capers*
Olive oil	*Sultana raisins*
Swordfish steak	*Lemon zest & juice*
Garlic	*Mint*
Cerignola olives (pitted)	*Parsley*

This dish is based on a Melissa Clark recipe from the *New York Times,* with our additions. Cut ½ lb. swordfish steak into slices about 2 inches long and sauté in the oil over high heat until light golden. Turn down the heat and add 2 good-sized cloves of sliced garlic. Sauté in the oil until translucent. *(Do not brown.)* Add 12 chopped olives, 2 dozen ★capers and ½ cup sultanas, using a bit of the boiling pasta water from time to time to keep the mixture moist. When the paccheri are just beyond *al dente* (about 15 minutes), drain, add to pan and stir in along with 1 tsp. lemon juice, ½ tsp. lemon zest, the minced mint, parsley and a bit more pasta water. Stir over high heat until the water is absorbed and the pasta glistens from the oil. Cover pan and bring to table.

(★Note: if the capers are packed in salt, rinse them well before using.)

December, Week 4

Linguine with lobster sauce

Ingredients:

Linguine	*Garlic*
Olive oil	*Tomatoes*
Lobster tail	*Parsley*
Sea salt & white pepper	

P.E. & D.D. Seafood still sells Long Island lobster. This is an alternate, simpler recipe than Ron's mother's, which his brother Richard still makes every Christmas Eve and which remains the standard. Heat the oil over medium-high heat. Add the lobster tail (½ cut lengthwise for each person), some ground sea salt and white pepper and sauté, shell side down, until red. Then turn and sauté over reduced heat for about 5 minutes. Remove from the oil and add 2 large cloves of pressed garlic. Sauté the garlic until translucent. *(Do not brown.)* Add 2 chopped tomatoes (fresh or frozen from the summer), sea salt and white pepper and sauté over high heat until reduced by about half. Meanwhile, remove the meat from the lobster tails and cut into ¼-inch pieces. Add back into the pan along with the shell halves and half the chopped parsley. Cover the pan and cook the sauce over low heat for 20–30 minutes until the lobster is tender. Add some boiling water from the pasta pot from time to time if needed. When the pasta is done, drain and add to the pan along with the remaining parsley, stirring until the sauce is absorbed and the pasta glistens with the oil. Cover pan and bring to table, garnishing each dish with a half lobster tail shell.

Appendix 1: Standard recipes

ARTICHOKES: To clean the artichokes, hold firmly in one hand, and with a sharp knife cut off the top third, removing the spines. Snap off the outer leaves until you reach the tender core. Quarter, cut out the chokes, leaving the hearts and only the most tender leaves. Toss into ice water and lemon to prevent the artichokes discoloring as you work.

ASPARAGUS: We use two sizes for our pasta dishes: the fatter ones if we are going to cream them, the thinner ones if we are going to cut and sauté. Snap off the woody lower one-quarter to one-third (wherever they look dry and pale). Remove any side scales with a sharp paring knife, then soak them in an oblong bowl to get out any sand or dirt. To sauté, first cut into 1-inch slices and parboil for 1-2 minutes.

To cream, cut the asparagus into 2- or 3-inch pieces. Boil just enough water in a small pot to cover the asparagus. Add the asparagus and cook until they feel tender when pierced with a fork — probably less than 5 minutes. Drain the asparagus, but preserve the water. Put the asparagus in a blender, add sea salt and milled white pepper and grind, adding a little of the cooking liquid to make it really smooth, but not watery.

BAKED ZITI AND CHEESE (À LA EDMUND GARDINER):
This involved very large amounts of sharp cheddar cheese and a little milk and butter in a sauce pan, cooking the pasta until relatively soft, and then baking everything until crispy and golden brown.

BEANS (DRIED WHITE, NAVY, CANNELLONI): Freshly dried white beans are like nothing you'll buy dry packaged or canned. Rinse well in a colander to remove any dust or small stones. Drop a cup into boiling salted water. Skim off any bean scum, turn the heat off and soak for several hours. Drain, add fresh water, some extra vergine oil, some milled white pepper, a pinch of salt and a bay leaf. Boil over low heat until tender.

CECI (DRIED CHICKPEAS, GARBANZOS): rinse the beans thoroughly in a colander, being careful to examine the contents for any small stones or other naturally occurring debris. Transfer to a pot of salted water and bring to a boil, removing any scum from the top. Drain, rinse, place in another pot of salted water and bring to a slow boil again for 60–90 minutes until the beans are *al dente*. Drain.

CHARD (from Deborah Madison, *Vegetarian Cooking for Everyone*):
2 large bunches chard (red, white, yellow or rainbow); about 2 lbs., leaves sliced into 1-inch wide ribbons; 1½ cups of chard stems trimmed and diced; 1 onion finely diced; ½ cup chopped cilantro; ⅓ cup olive oil; 1 tsp. paprika; 1 garlic clove pounded with 1 tsp. salt; salt and freshly milled pepper.

Place all ingredients in a wide, heavy pot with a few pinches of salt. Add ¼ cup water, cover tightly and cook over low heat for 45 minutes. Remove the chard and reduce the liquid to a rich, thick syrup. Add the chard back and coat thoroughly. When done, taste for salt and season with pepper. The chard should be silky and very fragrant.

CLAM SAUCE WITH LINGUINE (À LA EDMUND GARDINER):
1 can Progresso white clam sauce, 1 clove garlic, olive oil, 1 box linguine

This is pretty much how it was done in most kitchens into the 1970s. Heat the oil in a sauce pan. Add the garlic and soften until golden. Add the can of clam sauce and heat it through. Cook the pasta for exactly as long as it says on the box. Drain the pasta and top with all the sauce.

CRESPELLE (from Myra Waldo, *The Pancake Cookbook*):
4 eggs; ¾ cup milk; ¾ cup water; 1 cup sifted flour; ¾ tsp. salt; 3 tbsps. butter.

Beat eggs, stir in milk and water. Beat in the flour and salt until very smooth. Chill 30 minutes. The batter should be thin: add a little milk if necessary. Melt a little butter in a 6-inch skillet. Pour in just enough batter to coat the bottom thinly. Tilt the pan quickly as you pour. Cook until browned on one side. Flip and brown on the other side. Stack while cooking the remaining crespelle, adding butter to the skillet as needed.

Fava: These fresh beans (they can also be purchased dried, loose in barrels, canned or packaged), appear in heaps of fat, long pods at the end of Spring. Shell the fava by pulling the thin string on the inner seam and pressing open the shell with your thumb. Pop out the raw beans into a bowl. Discard any that are pale or shrivelled: they should all be bright green, whatever their size. Cook in a pot of boiling salted water for about 5 minutes. The outer shells of the shelled beans will now look a pale brown. Drain, run under cold water, then *pop* the beans out of their shells by pressing the end away from the dark nib. It's OK if some come out in halves or even smashed. They will look a very bright green.

Mixed pasta: Whenever we have a quantity of leftover (uncooked) *pasta secca,* too small to make two servings, we add it to a large Le Parfait jar. When that's full (usually 1-1½ lbs.), it's time for a *pasta al forno*.

Pecorino: we use Parmigiano more frequently, but since the Market cheese makers sell several varieties of pecorino and no Parmigiano, we use it here in the list of ingredients. You can easily substitute Parmigiano.

Pesto: Time was that we would do all this in a large mortar and pestle. Now we use a blender. Take 1 clove of garlic, a quarter cup of pine nuts, the basil, stems removed *(do not wet)* and run in a blender. When smooth and the basil is as small as possible, add the olive oil and parmigiano and blend again until the pesto forms a thick sauce. Move to a small serving bowl and add enough olive oil to cover.

RATATOUILLE (from Richard Olney, *Provence the Beautiful Cookbook):*
1 cup olive oil; 2 lbs. onions coarsely cut; 2 lbs. firm, glossy elongated eggplants, thickly sliced and then cut into large cubes; 2 lbs. red, yellow and green sweet peppers, halved lengthwise, seeded, de-ribbed and cut into squares; 2 lbs. ripe tomatoes, peeled, seeded and coarsely cut; 1 head garlic, cloves separated and peeled; large bouquet garni, *including celery, parsley, 3 bay leaves and several thyme sprigs; freshly ground pepper; fresh basil leaves.*

Warm half of the olive oil in an 8–10 qt. pot over low heat. Add onions and cook gently until softened, about 10 minutes. Stir occasionally with a wooden spoon as you begin to cut up and progressively add the rest of the vegetables. Add the salt and start gently scraping the bottom of the pot until the vegetables begin to release their liquid. Raise the heat to medium and bring to a boil. From the time the onions were added to the pot to the moment of when the boil is reached, 45 minutes to one hour should elapse.

Bury the *bouquet garni* beneath the vegetables, reduce the heat to maintain a light, bubbling simmer and cover with the lid slightly ajar. Simmer from 1 to 1¼ hours or until all the vegetables are tender. The vegetables must now be drained and their juices reduced. Place a large colander with legs into a heavy saucepan. Pour the contents of the pot into the colander. Let drain for a couple of minutes, then prop colander over empty bowl to continue draining.

Place the juices over a high heat, bring to a boil, and then reduce the heat to maintain a gentle boil. Keep adding the newly drained juices to the pot. About an hour will be required for the juices to reduce to a deep mahogany-colored syrup with a foamy boil. Toward the end of the reduction, survey the pan constantly, stirring often, and remove it from the heat the moment the foamy oil begins to subside to a staccato bubble.

Return the vegetables to the cooking pot, remove the *bouquet garni* and pour in the reduced juices, scraping the pot clean. Gently stir the vegetables until evenly coated with reduced juices. Turn them into a large dish to cool. Grind over some pepper and stir several spoonfuls of the remaining olive oil into the cooled vegetables. Tear basil leaves into fragments and scatter over the top. Serve at room temperature. Refrigerate any leftovers.

RAVIOLI AND TOMATO SAUCE (À LA EDMUND GARDINER):
1 can tomato puree, 1 can tomato paste, 1 onion, 1 clove garlic, olive oil, 1 box large cheese ravioli

Heat the oil in a sauce pan. Add the garlic and onions and sauté until well browned. Remove the onions and garlic and discard. Add the tomato paste and stir it around for a while, then add the tomato puree and salt and pepper. Cook for hours. Cook the pasta for exactly as long as it says on the box. Drain the pasta and top with all the sauce that can possibly fit in the bowl.

SALSA ANCONETANA (from Ada Boni, *Italian Regional Cooking*): This is the sauce created by baking *Stoccafisso all'Anconetana*. It's baked in layers.
Use about 2½ lbs. soaked salt cod and 4 potatoes sliced thin. Make the sauce (olive oil, ¾ lb. tomatoes, 1 carrot, 1 stalk celery, 1 finely chopped onion, 2 cloves of garlic sliced, some thyme). In an oiled ceramic baking dish put a layer of thinly sliced potato, a layer of salted cod, a layer of sauce, and repeat to 3 layers. Then add about 1 cup olive oil and ½ cup milk, and bake at about 375° F until the top is browned (45 minutes to an hour) and the sauce thickens, but don't let it cook too long or it will dry out.

A Year in Union Square

SPAGHETTI AND MEATBALLS (À LA EDMUND GARDINER), with sausage option: Spaghetti was paired with meatballs, made from ground beef, pork and veal from the Italian butcher on Henry Street, near Kane. This recipe was sometimes embellished with sweet Italian sausage also from the same butcher.

Meatballs, about ½ inches in diameter using: 1 lb. chopped meat, 1 egg, a few pieces of stale bread soaked in water, salt and pepper.

For the sauce: meatballs, sausage (optional), 1 can chopped tomatoes, 1 can tomato paste, 1 onion, 1 clove garlic, olive oil, 1 box spaghetti.

Heat the oil in a sauce pan. Add the garlic and onions and sauté until dark brown. Remove the onions and garlic and discard. Brown the meatballs in batches and remove. Then, if you're including sausages, brown and then remove them. Add the tomato paste and stir it around for a while, then add the tomatoes and salt and pepper. Add back the meatballs (and sausage) and simmer for hours. Allow to stand refrigerated overnight. Cook the pasta for exactly as long as it says on the box. Drain the pasta and top with all the sauce that can possibly fit in the bowl.

VEGETABLE STOCK: Generally we follow Deborah Madison's *Vegetarian Cooking for Everyone* when making vegetable stock, but here's a list of the ingredients:

Always include onions, carrots, celery, garlic, parsley, bay leaf, thyme, salt, olive oil.

Include if you have them and like them or need them:

Leeks, chard stems and leaves, beet greens (except for red beet greens), scallions, fennel, tomatoes, sage, rosemary, marjoram, basil.

Cut the vegetables into chunks. Heat the oil in a large stock pot. Brown the vegetables. The longer they brown the richer the stock. After about ten minutes add salt. Stir and cook about 5 minutes longer. Add enough cold water to cover well. Bring to boil. Lower heat and simmer about 30 minutes. Strain the broth. If you're storing it for future use (i.e., freezing it), once you've removed the vegetables, condense the broth by bringing it to a rapid boil until the liquid is reduced by half.

Don't overcook the vegetables or the broth may become bitter. *Do <u>not</u> add the following to the stock:* turnips, rutabagas, cabbage, Brussels sprouts, onion skins, artichoke trimmings, powdered herbs, celery seeds, excessive greens, red beet greens unless you want a red stock, and anything you wouldn't eat.

ZUCCHINI BLOSSOMS: In Union Square we buy male zucchini blossoms from Windfall Farms. With a sharp knife cut gently around (not through) the blossom just above the line of sepals (the little green pointy leaves just below the petals). Once a clean cut all around is made, pull on the stem and remove both the sepals and the stamen. Check inside for little bugs who love the blossoms as much as we do. *(If you do find any, please release them out the window, so they can continue pollinating flowers.)* The blossoms won't keep too long in the refrigerator, so it's best to buy them within a day or two of when you want to use them.

Appendix 2: Metric Equivalents

All recipes in this book are in US measures, but here is a short list of common metric equivalents:

US	Metric
Pound (lb.) liquid	*.47 liter*
Pound (solid)	*.45 kilo*
Ounce (oz.)	*28 grams*
Quart (Qt.)	*1.14 liter*
Pint	*.55 liter*
Cup	*.2 liter*
Tablespoon (tbsp.)	*14 milliliter*
Teaspoon (tsp.)	*5 milliliter*
Inch	*2.54 centimeter*

Index of Pastas

Index of Ingredients

This index does not list common ingredients, such as olive oil, garlic, parsley, pecorino or pepperoncini, since they are used in almost every recipe.

This Book Was Completed on September 24, 2015 at
The Pierrepont Street Press in New York, New York.
It Was Set in Adobe Bembo and Bembo Expert.
This Print Edition Was Produced
On 70-lb White Paper
in the USA and
Worldwide.

CPSIA information can be obtained at www.ICGtesting.com
Printed in the USA
BVIW12n1210171215
427424BV00003B/13

9 781599 103174